New Life Clarity Publishing
205 West 300 South, Brigham City, Utah 84302

Http://newlifeclarity.com/

Printed in the United States of America
ISBN- 978-1-0881-9358-7

DETAILS! DETAILS! DETAILS! WRITING YOUR FIRST BOOK

By
Pattie Godfrey~Sadler

ABOUT THE AUTHOR

Founder & CEO of New Life Clarity Publishing, (newlifeclarity.com) and Vice President of LA Tribune Publishing, Pattie Godfrey-Sadler adds her passion of sharing voices to inspire others for healing to the world. International Best Selling Author, Speaker, Retreat Facilitator and Influencer, her mission is to create transformation on all levels so that writers can achieve their highest of achievements. Guaranteed bestselling author programs, Author Academy, transformative retreats, and all kinds of programs are offered when working with New Life Clarity Publishing.

Pattie Godfrey-Sadler has a talent for motivating others and inspiring others to find the big WHY in their own lives to embark on the adventure called authorship. First responder and gifted trainer, she assists business owners, sales teams, entrepreneurs, and authors to find unexpected and amazing results.

Talk Show Host, Creator of HeartTalks, Savvy Retreat Facilitator, she truly lives life with passion and has shown that it is possible to create life changing results. She offers consulting to assist others to manifest their life vision as an author and influencer to become a reality. An expert in life changing and transition, she can assist you to declare just where you are going and create it!

Pattie Godfrey~Sadler
CEO/Founder New Life Clarity Publishing

DEDICATION

I created this to help all the amazing authors with amazing stories who deserve to be read!

Your heart has been felt and needs to be shared with the world. Write your book! You can do it!

TABLE OF CONTENTS

Chapter 1

GETTING STARTED

Writing a book is a long and challenging process, but it can also be incredibly rewarding. If you are thinking about writing a book, here are a few things to keep in mind:

1. **Start with an idea.** The first step in writing a book is to come up with an idea. This could be a story you have always wanted to tell, a topic you are passionate about, or a unique perspective you want to share with the world. Once you have an idea, it is important to flesh it out and develop it into a strong concept.

2. **Do your research.** Before you start writing, it is important to do your research. This means reading books and articles on your topic, talking to experts, and gathering as much information as you can. The more research you do the more informed and confident your writing will be.

3. **Create an outline.** Once you have a good understanding of your topic, it is time to create an outline. This will help you organize your thoughts and ensure that your book has a clear structure. Your outline should include the main points you want to make, as well as the supporting evidence you will use.

4. **Start writing.** The hardest part of writing a book is actually starting to write. However, do not worry; you don't have to write the entire book in one sitting. Just start by writing a few paragraphs or pages, and then gradually build up from there. The important thing is to just keep writing.

5. **Edit and revise.** Once you have a draft of your book, it is important to edit and revise it. This means checking for errors, making sure your writing is clear and concise, and polishing your prose. Don't worry about making it perfect at this stage, just focus on making it the best it can be.

6. **Get feedback.** Once you are happy with your book, it's a good idea to get feedback from others. This could be from friends, family, beta readers, or even a professional editor. Feedback can help you identify areas that need improvement and make sure your book is ready for publication.

7. **Find a publisher.** If you are planning to self-publish your book, you will need to find a publisher. This could be an online publisher, a print-on-demand publisher, or even a vanity press. Once you have found a publisher, they will help you with the rest of the process, such as editing, design, and marketing.

8. **Promote your book.** Once your book is published, it is important to promote it. This could involve creating a website for your book, running social media ads, or attending book signings. The more you promote your book, the more likely it is to be successful.

Writing a book is a lot of work, but it is also incredibly rewarding. If you have a story to tell or a message to share, don't be afraid to put it out there. The world is waiting to hear from you.

Tips for getting started

Here are a few tips for getting started on your book:

- **Set aside time to write.** The best way to make progress on your book is to set aside time to write each day. Even if it is just for 30 minutes, make sure you are carving out some time to work on your book.

- **Find a quiet place to write.** When you are trying to focus on writing, it is important to find a quiet place where you will not be interrupted. This could be a library, a coffee shop, or even your own bedroom.

- **Get organized.** Before you start writing, it is important to get organized. This means creating an outline, gathering your research, and setting up a writing space. The more organized you are, the less time you will spend fumbling around and the more time you will spend writing.

- **Do not be afraid to make mistakes.** Everyone makes mistakes when they are writing. The important thing is to not let your mistakes stop you from writing. Just keep writing and you'll eventually get it right.

- **Celebrate your progress.** As you make progress on your book, it›s important to celebrate your successes. This could mean rewarding yourself with a treat, or simply taking some time to reflect on your progress. Celebrating your progress will help you stay motivated and on track.

Chapter 2

GETTING ORGANIZED

Getting Organized

Writing a book is a big undertaking, and it is important to be organized from the start. This will help you stay on track and make the process more manageable. There are a few different ways to get organized when writing a book.

Create an Outline

One of the best ways to get organized is to create an outline. This will help you map out your book and make sure all of the pieces fit together. When creating an outline, be sure to include the following:

- The main points you want to make

- The supporting evidence you will use

- The order in which you want to present your material

Gather Your Research

Once you have an outline, you can start gathering your research. This will help you flesh out your ideas and make your book more informative. When gathering research, be sure to use a variety of sources, including books, articles, websites, and interviews.

Set Up a Writing Space

Another important part of getting organized is setting up a writing space. This will help you focus and get into the writing zone. When setting up a writing space, be sure to include the following:

- A comfortable chair

- A desk

- A quiet place

- All of your writing materials

Get into a Routine

Once you have everything in place, it is time to get into a routine. This means setting aside time each day to write, and sticking to that schedule as much as possible. It is also important to find a time of day when you are most productive. Some people prefer to write early in the morning, while others prefer to write late at night.

Don't Be Afraid to Take Breaks

It is also important to take breaks when you are writing. This will help you avoid burnout and stay focused. When taking a break, be sure to do something that does not involve screens, such as taking a walk or reading a book.

Celebrate Your Progress

As you make progress on your book, be sure to celebrate your successes. This could mean rewarding yourself with a treat, or simply taking some time to reflect on your progress. Celebrating your progress will help you stay motivated and on track.

Don't Give Up

Writing a book is a long and challenging process, but it is also incredibly rewarding. If you are struggling, do not give up. Just keep writing and eventually you will reach your goal.

Getting Organized is the Key to Success

Getting organized is the key to success when writing a book. By taking the time to create an outline, gather your research, and set up a writing space, you'll be well on your way to writing a great book.

Chapter 3

DO YOUR RESEARCH

Doing Your Research

Research is an essential part of writing a book. By doing your research, you can ensure that your book is well informed and accurate. There are a few different ways to do research for your book.

Primary Research

Primary research is research that you conduct yourself. This could involve interviewing experts, conducting surveys, or conducting experiments. Primary research can be a lot of work, but it is also the most rewarding. By conducting your own research, you can get the information you need firsthand and ensure that your book is accurate.

Secondary Research

Secondary research is research that you conduct by using information that has already been collected by others. This could involve reading books and articles, watching documentaries, or listening to podcasts. Secondary research can be a great way to get a general overview of a topic, but it is important to be careful about the sources you use. Not all information is created equal, and some sources may be more reliable than others.

Evaluating Your Research

Once you have done your research, it is important to evaluate it. This means assessing the quality of your sources and making sure that the information you have gathered is accurate and reliable. There are a few different ways to evaluate your research.

Check Your Sources

The first step in evaluating your research is to check your sources. Make sure that your sources are credible and that they provide accurate information. You can check the credibility of a source by looking at the author's credentials, the publication date, and the source's reputation.

Crosscheck Your Information

Once you have checked your sources, it is important to crosscheck your information. This means comparing the information from different sources to make sure it is consistent. If you find that the information from different sources is inconsistent, you may need to do more research to find out which information is accurate.

Be Critical of Your Information

It's also important to be critical of your information. Just because something is in print or online does not mean it is true. Be sure to think critically about the information you have gathered and make sure it makes sense.

Using Your Research

Once you have evaluated your research, you can start using it in your book. Be sure to cite your sources properly and give credit where credit is due.

Using your research will help you write a well-informed and accurate book.

Tips for Doing Your Research

Here are a few tips for doing your research:

1. **Start early.** Don›t wait until the last minute to start doing your research. The earlier you start, the more time you›ll have to find the information you need and evaluate it.

2. **Be organized.** Keep track of your research as you do it. This will help you avoid losing important information and make it easier to find what you need later.

3. **Be patient.** Doing research can be a time-consuming process. Do not get discouraged if you don't find the information you need right away. Just keep looking and you'll eventually find what you're looking for.

4. **Be open-minded.** Don›t be afraid to change your mind as you do your research. If you find information that contradicts your original ideas, be willing to adjust your thinking.

5. **Have fun!** Doing research can be a lot of fun. Enjoy the process of learning about your topic and discovering new information.

Chapter 4

CREATE AN OUTLINE

An outline is a tool that helps you organize your thoughts and ideas for your book. It can be a simple list of topics, or it can be a more detailed roadmap that includes the main points you want to make, the supporting evidence you will use, and the order in which you want to present your material.

There are many different ways to create an outline. Some people prefer to start by brainstorming a list of topics, while others prefer to start by developing a thesis statement and then building the outline around that. There is no right or wrong way to create an outline, as long as it works for you.

Here are a few tips for creating an effective outline:

- **Start with a thesis statement.** A thesis statement is a sentence that summarizes the main point of your book. Once you have a thesis statement, you can use it to develop the outline.

- **Break down your main points.** Once you have a thesis statement, you can break down your main points into smaller sub points. This will help you organize your thoughts and make sure that your outline is well structured.

- **Use evidence to support your points.** When you make a point in your outline, be sure to provide evidence to support it. This could be evidence from your research, from your personal experience, or from the work of others.

- **Organize your outline in a logical order.** The order in which you present your material in your outline should be logical. This means that you should start with the most basic information and then work your way up to the more complex information.

Creating an outline can be a lot of work, but it is an essential step in the writing process. By taking the time to create an outline, you can ensure that your book is well organized and that your ideas flow smoothly.

Here are some benefits of creating an outline:

- **It helps you organize your thoughts and ideas.** An outline can help you gather your thoughts and ideas and organize them into a cohesive whole. This can be especially helpful if you are writing a long or complex book.

- **It helps you stay on track.** An outline can help you stay on track as you write your book. By having a clear plan in place, you are less likely to be sidetracked or lose your way.

- **It helps you identify any gaps in your research.** An outline can help you identify any gaps in your research. As you develop your outline, you may realize that you need to do more research on certain topics.

- **It helps you write a more effective book.** An outline can help you write a more effective book. By having a clear plan in place, you are more likely to write a book that is well structured and easy to follow.

If you are serious about writing a book, then creating an outline is an essential step. By taking the time to create an outline, you can ensure that your book is well organized and that your ideas flow smoothly.

Chapter 5

START WRITING

The most important step in writing a book is to start writing. Once you have an outline and have done your research, it is time to start putting words on paper (or on your computer screen).

Here are a few tips for getting started:

- **Just start writing.** Don›t worry about making it perfect. Just start writing and see what happens. You can always go back and edit later.

- **Write in a place where you feel comfortable.** Some people prefer to write in a quiet place, while others prefer to write in a more chaotic environment. Find a place where you feel comfortable and where you can focus on your writing.

- **Set a goal for yourself.** Decide how much you want to write each day or each week. Having a goal will help you stay on track and make progress towards finishing your book.

- **Do not be afraid to make mistakes.** Everyone makes mistakes when they are writing. The important thing is to not let your mistakes stop you from writing. Just keep writing and you will eventually get it right.

- **Celebrate your progress.** As you make progress on your book, be sure to celebrate your successes. This could mean rewarding yourself with a treat, or simply taking some time to reflect on your progress. Celebrating your progress will help you stay motivated and on track.

Writing a book is a lot of work, but it is also an incredibly rewarding experience. By following these tips, you can make the process a little bit easier and a little bit more fun.

Tips for Staying Motivated

Here are a few tips for staying motivated when writing your book:

- **Set realistic goals.** Do not try to write the entire book in one sitting. Set realistic goals for yourself, such as writing a certain number of pages or chapters per day.

- **Take breaks.** Do not try to write for hours on end without taking a break. Get up and move around every 20-30 minutes. This will help you stay focused and avoid burnout.

- **Find a writing buddy.** Having a writing buddy can help you stay motivated. You can meet up with your writing buddy regularly to discuss your progress and offer each other support.

- **Join a writing group.** There are many writing groups available, both online and in person. Joining a writing group can help you stay motivated and connected with other writers.

- **Read other books.** Reading other books can help you stay motivated and inspired. When you read a great book, it can make you want to write your own great book.

- **Remember your why.** Why are you writing this book? What do you hope to achieve with it? Keeping your why in mind can help you stay motivated when the going gets tough.

Writing a book is a long and challenging process, but it is also an incredibly rewarding experience. By following these tips, you can make the process a little bit easier and a little bit more fun.

Chapter 6

REVISING YOUR BOOK

Once you have a first draft of your book, it's time to start revising and rewriting. This is where you will polish your prose, correct any errors, and make your book the best it can be.

1. Revise your book

Revising is the process of making changes to your book to improve its overall structure and content. When revising, you may want to consider the following:

- **The overall structure of your book.** Does your book have a clear beginning, middle, and end? Is the structure logical and easy to follow?

- **The content of your book.** Are your ideas clear and well supported? Is the information accurate and up-to-date?

- **The style of your writing.** Is your writing clear and easy to read? Is your language engaging and interesting?

2. Rewriting your book

Rewriting is the process of making changes to your book at the sentence level. When rewriting, you may want to consider the following:

- **The clarity of your writing.** Are your sentences clear and easy to understand? Do you use active voice and specific verbs?

- **The flow of your writing.** Does your writing flow smoothly from one sentence to the next? Do you use transition words and phrases to help the reader follow your train of thought?

- **The rhythm of your writing.** Does your writing have a natural rhythm? Do you use repetition and alliteration to create a pleasing sound?

Tips for Revising and Rewriting

Here are a few tips for revising and rewriting:

- **Read your book aloud.** Reading your book aloud can help you identify any areas that need improvement.

- **Get feedback from others.** Ask friends, family, or beta readers to read your book and give you feedback.

- **Use a writing style guide.** A writing style guide can help you identify and correct any errors in your writing.

- **Take breaks.** Do not try to revise and rewrite your book in one sitting. Take breaks when you need them and come back to your book with fresh eyes.

- **Do not be afraid to make changes.** The goal of revising and rewriting is to make your book the best it can be. Do not be afraid to make changes, even if they are major changes.

Revising and rewriting can be a lot of work, but it is an essential part of the writing process. By taking the time to revise and rewrite your book, you can make it the best it can be.

Chapter 7

GETTING FEEDBACK

Getting feedback on your book is an important part of the writing process. Feedback can help you identify areas that need improvement, as well as get suggestions for how to make your book better.

There are a few different ways to get feedback on your book. You can ask friends, family, or beta readers to read your book and give you feedback. You can also join a writing group or online forum and get feedback from other writers.

When you ask for feedback, be sure to be specific about what you are looking for. Do you want feedback on the overall structure of your book? The content? The style? Be sure to give your readers some guidance so that they can give you the most helpful feedback.

Once you have received feedback, be sure to take the time to read it and consider it. Even if you don't agree with all of the feedback you receive, it can still be helpful in identifying areas that need improvement.

Getting feedback can be a lot of work, but it is an essential part of the writing process. By taking the time to get feedback, you can make your book the best it can be.

Tips for Getting Feedback

Here are a few tips for getting feedback:

- **Be specific about what you are looking for.** When you ask for feedback, be sure to be specific about what you are looking for. Do you want feedback on the overall structure of your book? The content? The style? Be sure to give your readers some guidance so that they can give you the most helpful feedback.

- **Be open to feedback.** Even if you don›t agree with all of the feedback you receive, it can still be helpful in identifying areas that need improvement.

- **Be willing to make changes.** If you receive feedback that suggests that you need to make changes to your book, be willing to make those changes. Even if the changes are major, they may be necessary to make your book the best it can be.

- **Thank your readers for their feedback.** Even if you don›t use all of the feedback you receive, be sure to thank your readers for their time and effort. Feedback is a gift, and it is important to appreciate it.

Chapter 8

FINDING A PUBLISHER

Once you have a finished manuscript, the next step is to find a publisher. There are two main ways to do this:

1. **Submit your manuscript to traditional publishers.** Traditional publishers are the big companies that publish the majority of books. To submit your manuscript to a traditional publisher, you will need to create a query letter and a synopsis. Your query letter should introduce your book and explain why you think it would be a good fit for the publisher. Your synopsis should give a brief overview of your book, including the plot, characters, and setting.

2. **Self-publish your book.** Self-publishing means that you will be responsible for publishing your book yourself. This can be a lot of work, but it also gives you more control over your book. To self-publish your book, you will need to create a cover, format your book, and distribute it to bookstores and online retailers.

Tips for Finding a Publisher

Here are a few tips for finding a publisher:

- **Do your research.** Before you submit your manuscript, be sure to do your research and find publishers that are a good fit for your book. You can find information about publishers online or in industry directories.

- **Write a strong query letter.** Your query letter is your first chance to make a good impression on a publisher. Be sure to write a strong letter that will grab the publisher›s attention and make them want to read your manuscript.

- **Get feedback on your manuscript.** Once you have a finished manuscript, be sure to get feedback from beta readers and other writers. This feedback can help you identify areas that need improvement and make your book the best it can be.

- **Be patient.** Finding a publisher can take time. Don›t get discouraged if you don›t get an offer right away. Just keep submitting your manuscript and eventually you will find a publisher who is a good fit for your book.

Pros and Cons of Self-Publishing

There are both pros and cons to self-publishing. Some of the pros include:

- **You have more control over your book.** When you self-publish, you have the final say on everything from the cover design to the pricing.

- **You can earn more money.** When you self-publish, you keep all of the royalties from your book sales.

- **Your book can be available to readers more quickly.** When you self-publish, you can get your book into readers› hands right away.

- Some of the cons include:

- **It can be a lot of work.** Self-publishing requires a lot of time and effort. You will need to create a cover, format your book, and distribute it to bookstores and online retailers.

- **You may not get as much exposure.** Self-published books are often not as well-known as traditionally published books.

- **You may not earn as much money.** Self-published books typically sell for less than traditionally published books.

Ultimately, the decision of whether to self-publish or submit to a traditional publisher is a personal one. There is no right or wrong answer. The best option for you will depend on your specific circumstances and goals.

Chapter 9

PROMOTING YOUR BOOK

Once you have written and published your book, it is important to promote it so that people can find it and read it. There are many different ways to promote your book, and the best approach for you will depend on your budget, your target audience, and your goals.

1. Online Marketing

There are many ways to promote your book online. You can create a website for your book, post about it on social media, and run online advertising campaigns.

Your website should be a hub for all of your book-related information. It should include a description of your book, a sample chapter, and links to where people can buy it. You can also use your website to connect with readers and build a community around your book.

Social media is a great way to connect with potential readers and promote your book. You can post about your book on your social media pages, run contests and giveaways, and engage with other users.

Online advertising can be a great way to reach a larger audience with your book promotion efforts. You can run ads on websites, social media platforms, and search engines.

2. Offline Marketing

There are also many ways to promote your book offline. You can give presentations at libraries, bookstores, and other venues. You can also sign copies of your book at events.

When giving presentations, be sure to have a copy of your book available for people to purchase. You can also use your presentations to generate interest in your book and drive people to your website or social media pages.

Signing copies of your book at events is a great way to meet potential readers and promote your book. Be sure to have a supply of books on hand, and be prepared to answer questions about your book.

3. Public Relations

Public relations can be a great way to generate interest in your book and get media coverage for it. You can contact journalists and bloggers who might be interested in reviewing your book or you can submit your book to awards and competitions.

When contacting journalists and bloggers, be sure to send them a copy of your book and a press release. Your press release should include a brief overview of your book, your contact information, and any awards or competitions your book has been nominated for.

Submitting your book to awards and competitions can be a great way to get recognition for your work and generate interest in your book. Many awards and competitions have deadlines, so be sure to check the deadlines before submitting your book.

Tips for Promoting Your Book

Here are a few tips for promoting your book:

- **Start early.** The earlier you start promoting your book, the more time you will have to reach your target audience.

- **Be consistent.** Promoting your book should be an ongoing effort. Do not just promote it once and then forget about it.

- **Be creative.** There are many different ways to promote your book. Be creative and come up with new and innovative ways to get the word out about your book.

- **Be patient.** Promoting your book takes time. Do not expect to see results overnight. Just keep promoting your book and eventually you will see results.

Chapter 10

CELEBRATE YOUR SUCCESS

Once you have finished writing your book and seen it through the publishing process, it is time to celebrate your success!

There are many different ways to celebrate your success. You can throw a party, give yourself a gift, or simply take some time to relax and enjoy your accomplishment.

1. Throw a party

One great way to celebrate your success is to throw a party. You can invite your friends, family, and anyone else who has supported you along the way. You can also invite other writers or people who are interested in your book.

At your party, you can serve food and drinks, play games, and just have a good time. You can also give a speech about your book and your journey to success.

2. Give yourself a gift

Another great way to celebrate your success is to give yourself a gift. This could be anything from a new piece of writing equipment to a trip to a place you have always wanted to visit.

The gift you give yourself should be something that you will enjoy and that will make you feel good about your accomplishment.

3. Take some time to relax

Finally, one of the best ways to celebrate your success is to simply take some time to relax and enjoy your accomplishment. This could mean taking a day off from work, reading a book, or taking a nap.

Whatever you do, make sure to take some time for yourself to relax and celebrate your success. You have earned it!

Tips for Celebrating Your Success

Here are a few tips for celebrating your success:

- **Make it personal.** Your celebration should be something that is meaningful to you. Don›t just do something because you feel like you have to.

- **Make it fun.** Celebrating your success should be enjoyable. If you are not having fun, then you are doing it wrong.

- **Make it inclusive.** Invite the people who have helped you along the way. They deserve to celebrate your success with you.

- **Make it memorable.** Do something that you will remember for years to come. Make your celebration special.

Milton Keynes UK
Ingram Content Group UK Ltd.
UKHW050006170224
437951UK00015B/832